Ravens

AJ Knight

Explore other books at:
WWW.ENGAGEBOOKS.COM

VANCOUVER, B.C.

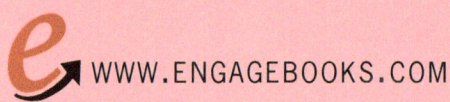 WWW.ENGAGEBOOKS.COM

Ravens: Level 3
Animals That Make a Difference!
Knight, AJ,
Text © 2024 Engage Books
Design © 2024 Engage Books

Edited by: A.R. Roumanis,
Sarah Harvey, Melody Sun, and Ashley Lee
Design by: Mandy Christiansen

Text set in Arial Regular.
Chapter headings set in Nathaniel-19.

FIRST EDITION / FIRST PRINTING

All rights reserved. No part of this book may be stored in a retrieval system, reproduced or transmitted in any form or by any other means without written permission from the publisher or a licence from the Canadian Copyright Licensing Agency. Critics and reviewers may quote brief passages in connection with a review or critical article in any media.

Every reasonable effort has been made to contact the copyright holders of all material reproduced in this book.

LIBRARY AND ARCHIVES CANADA CATALOGUING IN PUBLICATION

Title: Ravens / AJ Knight.
Names: Knight, AJ, author.
Description: Series statement: Animals that make a difference

Identifiers: Canadiana (print) 20230448623 | Canadiana (ebook) 20230448631
ISBN 978-1-77476-840-2 (hardcover)
ISBN 978-1-77476-841-9 (softcover)
ISBN 978-1-77476-842-6 (epub)
ISBN 978-1-77476-843-3 (pdf)
ISBN 978-1-77878-137-7 (audio)

Subjects:
LCSH: Ravens—Juvenile literature.
LCSH: Human-animal relationships—Juvenile literature.

Classification: LCC QL696.P2367 K65 2024 | DDC J598.8/64—DC23

This project has been made possible in part by the Government of Canada.

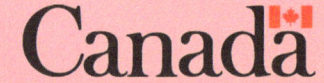

Contents

- 4   What Are Ravens?
- 6   A Closer Look
- 8   Where Do Ravens Live?
- 10   What Do Ravens Eat?
- 12   How Do Ravens Talk to Each Other?
- 14   Raven Life Cycle
- 16   Curious Facts About Ravens
- 18   Kinds of Ravens
- 20   How Ravens Help Earth
- 22   How Ravens Help Other Animals
- 24   How Ravens Help Humans
- 26   Ravens in Danger
- 28   How to Help Ravens
- 30   Quiz

What Are Ravens?

Ravens are black **songbirds** that people sometimes think are crows. They have larger beaks than crows. They are also bigger and have diamond-shaped tail feathers instead of rounded tail feathers.

Ravens are part of a group of songbirds called corvids. These birds are strong and smart. Ravens can solve problems and make plans for the future.

Songbirds: birds that sing songs.

A Closer Look

Ravens come in many different sizes. They can be between 18 and 26 inches (46 to 66 centimeters) long. They can weigh between 1 and 3.5 pounds (0.5 and 1.6 kilograms).

Ravens have long feathers at the ends of their wings. This makes it look like they have fingers.

Ravens have shaggy feathers near their throats. These shaggy throat feathers are called hackles.

Ravens' feet have three toes facing forward and one toe facing backward.

Where Do Ravens Live?

Ravens do not like to live near people. They live in mountains, deserts, and forests or near the sea. They live in nests made of sticks, bark, and hair. Their nests are found high up in trees or on cliffs.

Some ravens build nests that are 5 feet (1.5 meters) across.

Ravens can be found all over the world. Little ravens are only found in Australia. Chihuahuan ravens live in the Southwest US and northern Mexico. Thick-billed ravens can be found in eastern Africa.

What Do Ravens Eat?

Ravens are omnivores. This means they eat both plants and animals. They often eat small **mammals**, eggs, berries, and birds.

Ravens will also eat food that was killed by another animal. They even eat animals that have been hit by a car. Some ravens will look for food in landfills. These are places where garbage is collected and buried.

KEY WORD

Mammals: animals with warm blood and bones in their backs.

Ravens often hide their food away to eat later.

How Do Ravens Talk to Each Other?

Ravens make over 30 different sounds. Their deep croak is most common and can be heard from over a mile away. Other ravens will often call back if they hear this sound.

Ravens can learn to copy the sounds of other birds, dogs, and sirens.

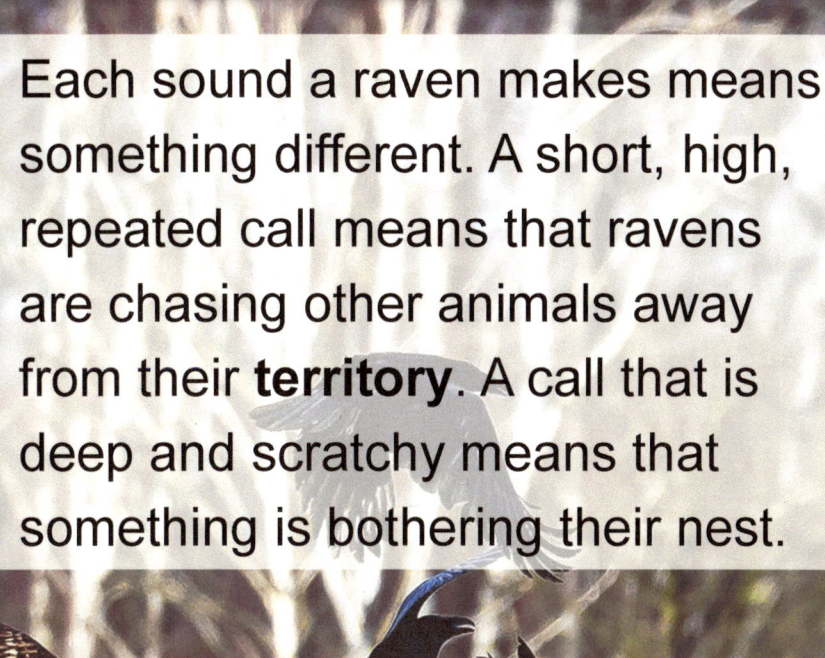

Each sound a raven makes means something different. A short, high, repeated call means that ravens are chasing other animals away from their **territory**. A call that is deep and scratchy means that something is bothering their nest.

KEY WORD

Territory: an area that an animal lives in and protects from other animals.

Raven Life Cycle

Female ravens lay between three and seven eggs at once. They sit on the eggs to keep them warm. The eggs hatch after about 20 days.

Baby ravens are called chicks. It takes about five weeks for them to grow all their feathers. They leave the nest shortly after this.

Ravens find a partner to start a family with when they are two to four years old. Most ravens stay with their partner for their whole lives. This partner is called their mate.

Most ravens live for 10 to 15 years in the wild. They can live much longer if cared for by humans. Some ravens have lived as long as 40 or 50 years.

Curious Facts About Ravens

Ravens can learn human words if they live close to people.

If a raven looks in a mirror, it knows it is looking at itself.

Ravens can remember people's faces.

A raven's feathers are shiny and sometimes look green, blue, or purple.

Ravens will comfort their friends if they lose a fight.

Ravens sometimes play in the snow.

Kinds of Ravens

There are about ten different kinds of ravens. The common raven lives in more places around the world than any other raven. They can be over 4 feet (1.3 meters) wide from one wing tip to the other.

Brown-necked ravens are brown and black. They sometimes work as a team to hunt lizards.

Australian ravens are born with dark eyes. Their eyes turn white when they become adults.

White-necked ravens have thick bills. They also have shorter tails than most ravens.

How Ravens Help Earth

Ravens often bury seeds underground so they can come back and eat them later. Sometimes ravens forget where their seeds are buried. This allows the seeds to grow into new plants.

Ravens also help make sure only the healthiest plants grow. They study seeds before burying them to make sure there are no bugs or **fungi** inside. Seeds with bugs or fungi in them will grow into unhealthy plants.

KEY WORD

Fungi: a group of living things that are not plants or animals.

How Ravens Help Other Animals

Ravens work with other animals to hunt large animals. Ravens will call to a pack of wolves when they see large **prey**. The wolves will then hunt the animal. The ravens pick at what is left after the wolves are done eating.

KEY WORD

Prey: an animal that is hunted and eaten by another animal.

Young ravens can also be a food source for other birds. Hawks, eagles, and owls all hunt young ravens. They do not usually hunt adult ravens.

Ravens are known as "wolf birds" by some people.

How Ravens Help Humans

Ravens help people save money. **Conservation** groups often have to pay people to plant trees. Ravens do this job for free. Conservation groups can then use this money for other things.

> **KEY WORD**
> **Conservation:** protecting and taking care of things found in nature.

Oxygen is a gas that people need to breathe. Trees make oxygen and help keep the air clean. By planting trees, ravens help make sure people have fresh, clean air to breathe.

Ravens in Danger

Ravens cannot always tell the difference between food and garbage. They often try to eat garbage they find on the ground. This can make them sick or cause them to die.

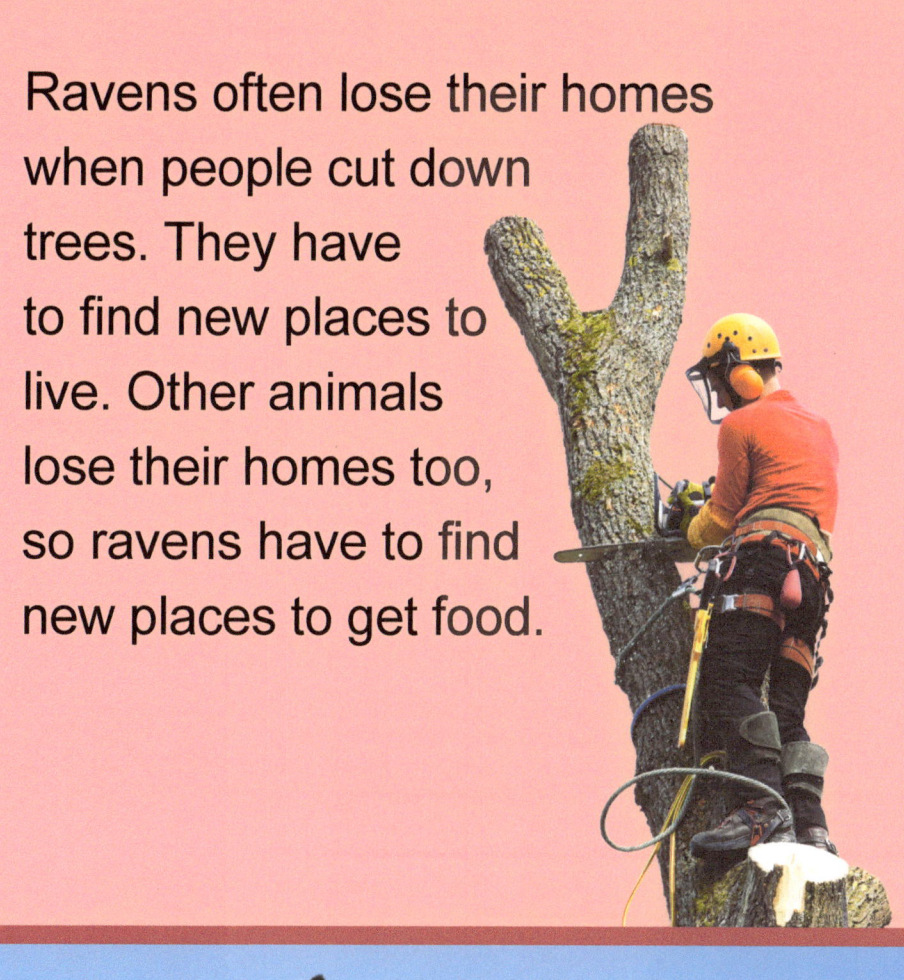

Ravens often lose their homes when people cut down trees. They have to find new places to live. Other animals lose their homes too, so ravens have to find new places to get food.

How to Help Ravens

Make sure to put your waste in the garbage and do not **litter**. This will help keep garbage away from ravens. You can also try to create less garbage by using containers instead of sandwich bags or metal straws instead of plastic ones.

KEY WORD

Litter: leave waste on the ground.

Make sure to stay away from raven nests. Ravens will sometimes attack people if they get too close to their nest. Staying away helps keep ravens from getting upset and helps keep you safe.

Quiz

Test your knowledge of ravens by answering the following questions. The questions are based on what you have read in this book. The answers are listed on the bottom of the next page.

1. What bird do people sometimes think ravens are?

2. What are a raven's shaggy throat feathers called?

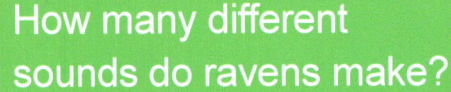

3. What are raven nests made out of?

4. How many different sounds do ravens make?

5. How long do ravens live for in the wild?

6. What can ravens learn if they live close to people?

Explore other books in the Animals That Make a Difference series

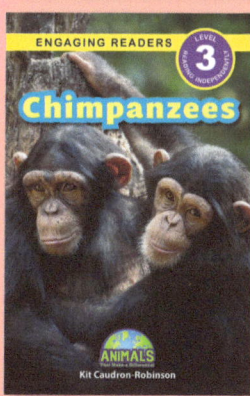
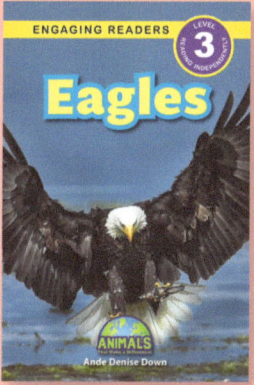
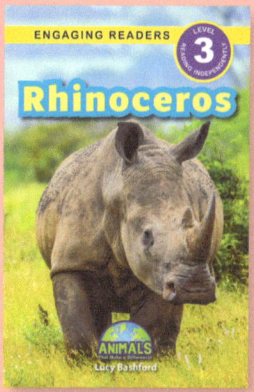

Visit www.engagebooks.com to explore more Engaging Readers.

Answers:
1. Crows 2. Hackles 3. Sticks, bark, and hair 4. Over 30 5. 10 to 15 years 6. Human words

31

Milton Keynes UK
Ingram Content Group UK Ltd.
UKHW051902300524
443359UK00001B/4